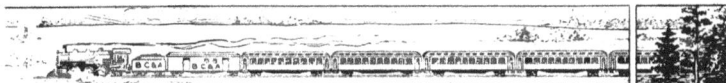

BALTIMORE, CHESAPEAKE AND ATLANTIC RAILWAY COMPANY

HERITAGE BOOKS
2008

HERITAGE BOOKS
AN IMPRINT OF HERITAGE BOOKS, INC.

Books, CDs, and more—Worldwide

For our listing of thousands of titles see our website
at
www.HeritageBooks.com

Published 2008 by
HERITAGE BOOKS, INC.
Publishing Division
100 Railroad Ave. #104
Westminster, Maryland 21157

International Standard Book Numbers
Paperbound: 978-1-58549-957-1
Clothbound: 978-0-7884-7612-9

Baltimore, Chesapeake & Atlantic Railway Co.

WILLARD THOMSON
Vice-President

T. MURDOCH
General Passenger Agent

General Offices:
PIER 1, PRATT STREET WHARF, BALTIMORE, MD.

Foreword

In common with all transportation litera-
ture, this booklet fares forth with a two-
fold purpose. Briefly, it is this: to encourage
patronage of the excellent resorts and
summering places on the rail and water
lines of the Baltimore, Chesapeake &
Atlantic and Maryland, Delaware & Virginia
Railway Companies, and at the same time
to serve the public as a guide to enjoyable outings and summer vacations.

Lists of hotels and boarding-houses are
appended, and should prove helpful to every
prospective vacationist.

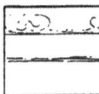

Ocean City, Maryland

Maryland's Only Ocean Resort--Quaint, Different and
Delightful--Its Beach Said by Many to be Super-
ior to Any on the Atlantic Coast--Situated
Midway Between Boston and Key
West--An Ideal Resort.

Vacation-time brings, besides many pleasant anticipa-
tions, a few perplexities. We are speaking, of course, for the
adults. Many, many details have to be considered by the
heads of a family before settling upon a definite plan for
the annual summer vacation, however brief it may be. If
the great event is to continue during the entire summer,
the importance of the preliminaries is increased many fold;
but even a fortnight's freedom beside the summer sea calls
for a deal of thoughtful planning. Absence from home
always brings its problems, but to locate comfortably and

attractively abroad, in vacation-time, is known sometimes
to bring problems of greater magnitude.

In telling you of Ocean City, Maryland, we shall ever
try to remember to be conservative. If our story be colored
a trifle with romance, we trust you will find it subdued
somewhat with the shadows of conservatism. We feel sure,
though, you would not have us close the door on Romance,
such an exquisite thing is she. And of a verity, what would
a sea-shore vacation be without her!

Ocean City was made for young men and maidens, and
the exuberance of their buoyant spirits looms large on the
beach and boardwalk from June till September. They find
such a wide variety of things to do, of diversions to occupy
their time, that "summer's sad farewell" comes weeks too
soon. Their elders, too, fall in line with the fun, because fun
is ever so contagious. Eyes that shone dull beneath gray
locks soon take on the sparkle of merriment and the lustre

The "Plimhimmon"

Getting "Kodaked" on the Boardwalk

of youth. Salt air does it—salt air and summer's sunshine and the every-day frolic with that nicest of play-fellows, the great billowing ocean.

About the Bathing

A gay sight it is to witness all ages and conditions of humanity at play in the surf of a modern seaside resort. Grizzled veterans become mere lads; matrons who have reached the decline and fall of their social empire, so to speak, disport themselves like winsome debutantes of scarce twenty summers; mere children approach old ocean's bristling surge with a glee that bespeaks affection—and all are merry together in the fulness of vacation's emancipation. Yes, it is good to watch the bathers on a sunny summer's day, but it is infinitely better to indulge with them. So tempting, indeed, is the brine, that one with difficulty resists its call. And it is without exception the nucleus of seaside charm. Were it not for the delights of surf bathing, seaside resorts would hardly attract the vast throng of pleasure and comfort seekers who annually frequent them.

In this respect Ocean City is especially blessed. The quality of the surf here, more than all else, has won for the

place its standing among seaboard resorts. And its excellence appears to have been heralded surprisingly far. All that can be said about it, though, is well deserved, and this publication feels justified in singing its praises with loud acclaim. So gently, gradually, does the beach recede; so slight is the undertow; so fine and compact is the sand, that one cannot help falling in love with Maryland's coastal diadem, better known as Ocean City. The ocean's brine, too, is of crystal purity at this point; by which we mean that none of the city sewerage is allowed to empty into the surf and pollute its pellucid depths. This condition does not exist at every coast resort, we are told.

Hotels and Cottages.

Summer life at Ocean City, except at two or three of the more conventional hotels, takes on a decidedly home-like aspect. At any one of the numberless cottages where the summer colony is provided for, one finds that cordial welcome and generous hospitality which constitute the greeting of every Southern homestead. It is a real pleasure to enter such a hospice, a heartfelt satisfaction akin to joy to remain there, and one seldom leaves without a twitching of the heart-strings. But let it be said that this sort of thing

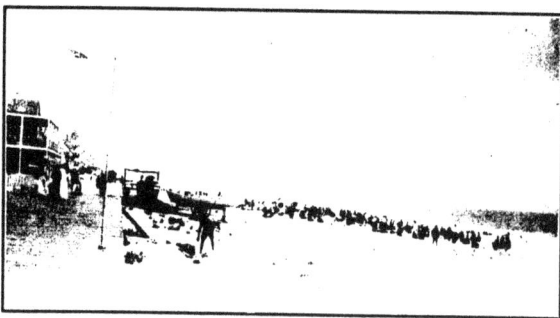

The Bathing Hour.

is epidemic in the South. Here folks just can't help being genial and hospitable once you have crossed their threshold. Assuming the guest be of the right sort, always he will find the "so-glad-to-see-you" and "so sorry-you're-leaving" attitude. And being of the South, in this, Ocean City is no exception.

Ocean City, Md., has not yet outgrown its need for the summer vacationist, and we hope it never will. If the vacationist needs Ocean City, far more is it true that Ocean City needs the vacationist. This fact accounts for that "so-glad-to-see-you" greeting which awaits you here.

Provincial? Well, no, not exactly. 'Tis true, Ocean City is little more than a seaside village during the winter months; but when summer begins to paint the westward landscape green, this coy little town by the sea, along with the Eastern Shore laurel and dogwood, begins to bloom out pretty soon, till, verily, a full-blown summer resort lifts its fragrance to the July sky.

And now, to speak again of such commonplace things as "board and lodging," let us plead with you, Mr. Vacationist, to refer to the list of Ocean City's hotels

and boarding-houses on page 38 of this book. Having done so, let us plead with you to exert yourself still further in behalf of your own comfort. Do this: Write a letter to one or to several of the houses on the list and ask them if they can accommodate you at a given time, state the sort of accommodations your heart desires, and ask for rates. Then, when you have received your replies, select the place that seems to suit you best and have your room or rooms reserved. By doing this you may save yourself many needless steps, and certainly much needless anxiety.

Sinepuxent Bay.

Sinepuxent Beach, on which Ocean City is built, is almost as fortunate on one side as on the other. Though washed on the eastward by the incomparable ocean, with all its magic charm, its western edge melts into the mellow waters of Sinepuxent Bay, that magnificent waterway for pleasure craft which trends the coast line fifty miles or more. Only those who have made the acquaintance of Sinepuxent Bay can really appreciate her merits. Truly her waters are rich with the touch of romantic suggestiveness, and you like to linger long upon them. The soft shimmering of the moonbeams casting their spell upon her bosom; the ripple and gurgle and gush of the million tiny wavelets; the refreshing salt of the air, fresh from the broad reaches of old Neptune—one and all easier felt than expressed—they greet you and create within you a warm sense of harmony when you seek your pleasure on the dream-waters of Sinepuxent. It matters not whether you are trusting your momentum to canvas, to the ubiquitous motor, or, and best of all, to the paddle of that captivating craft, the canoe, the charm of Sinepuxent besets you just the same.

Attractions of the Boardwalk

If the beach and surf rank first among the attractions of Ocean City, surely the boardwalk is a close rival for second place. Here, of a verity, one can hardly conceive

Section of the beach, showing pier in the distance.

how the summer populace would manage without this popular thoroughfare. It serves them as a promenade, as a rolling-chair boulevard, and as a variety show. It also serves somewhat as a common drawing-room, in which every summer visitor delights in playing the host to his chance acquaintances.

Ocean City's boardwalk has lately undergone some improvements. It is broader, smoother, and more substantial than it once was. Perhaps this is the reason why rolling-chairs have made their appearance during the past year or two. Anyhow, they are here, and so popular did they appear during the past season that there is little doubt they will remain.

Fishing and Crabbing

Present-day disciples of Isaak Walton, otherwise known as "lovers of pleasures piscatorial," will find the attractions of Ocean City particularly strong for them. Likewise are they varied. Not merely one, but many varieties of the finny tribe here await the cast of your bait. A few of the

more common varieties, we are told, are sea trout, kingfish, perch, bass, and bluefish. Many fish from the ocean pier, believing it to be the most effectual way of satisfying their angler's appetite. Others prefer Sinepuxent Bay, upon whose bosom they may sail far distances before casting the fly.

Now and then a vacationist of venturesome bent will brave the severity of old ocean's tossing and go in a small boat to sea to indulge his fisherman's taste. It usually follows, however, that those who are not inured to this experience find their legs a bit troublesome for a day or two after returning to terra firma, but this result seems only to add fun to the frolic for those who give it a try. It is hardly necessary to do this, however, as the pier extends quite far enough to afford most excellent deep-sea fishing.

Churches

Church-going vacationists will find at Ocean City sufficient churches to accommodate them. Two Protestant churches—a Presbyterian and an Episcopal—and a Catholic church comprise the list.

A glimpse of the Ocean Front.

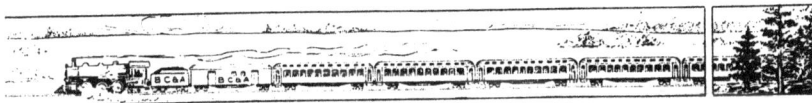

Artesian Water

Ocean City's water supply is worthy of mention. It is artesian and from great depth, and analysis shows that it is pure and wholesome. The importance of having good drinking water cannot be over-estimated. Baltimoreans can well appreciate this fact, because certainly their supply at home has been sadly deficient in quality during the past few years.

The Banner Year

Make your vacation of 1913 the greatest ever. Let this year be the banner year. Plan to spend it at Ocean City, Maryland, and enter into its rollicking fun with all the zest of which you are capable. Or just rest, if you prefer it, and from the cloister of your languor look out upon that pleasing spectacle of a host of city folks let loose beside the summer sea.

⋈　　⋈　　⋈

The old, old Story.

The Claiborne Cruise

**A Charming Little Cruise for Summer Afternoons---
Your Family Will Enjoy it---Your Best Girl
Will Adore it---Your Own Heart
Will Be Glad and Want
to Go Again.**

Summer brings down-the-bay trips. Indeed, Baltimoreans know no better way of spending an afternoon and evening pleasantly, enjoyably, than a trip on the grand old Chesapeake. They look forward to the coming of summer in delightful anticipation of the good times in the ''great outdoors'' which summer always brings.

The delights of the Chesapeake are acknowledged by everybody everywhere. Its broad, billowy bosom is swept

by cool refreshing breezes sizzling with salt. How allluring, then, must it be on a really warm day— a day when the atmosphere in town is a trifle sticky and oppressive! How one, at such times, yearns for a spin out over its flashing, splashing expanse! And it is a simple matter to have one's yearning gratified.

The Claiborne Cruise is at your service. It is one of the nicest down-the-bay trips leaving Baltimore. Its popularity has endured for many, many years. The expression "To Claiborne" is a by-word with Baltimoreans—one that is heard on every side during the warm midsummer months.

The Steamer "Cambridge" is the popular purveyor of this noted little voyage. She is trim, speedy, and in every way efficient, affording every reasonable comfort. She has room on every trip for 800 pleasure-seekers. She is loved by many old patrons of this line, and is worthy of all the favor and affection they may feel for her.

Her sailing time is 2.30 P. M. daily, except Sunday, from Pier 8, Light St., Baltimore. The trip lasts eight

On the Upper Chesapeake

hours, the return to Baltimore being about 10.30 P. M. On Sunday no afternoon trip is made on this line.

This trip means eight hours of jollification, of happy abandon, of gratifying relaxation. Yes, and it means a hefty appetite for supper—the supper the ship's dining-room provides —and it is usually a good one. The colored cooks of the Chesapeake are famous for the delicious meals they prepare, and their fame has traveled surprisingly far. They know the art of dressing the well-known Chesapeake Bay delicacies as only a native-born cook can know it. And pleasure-seekers on the Claiborne Cruise are given the benefit of their skill in this direction.

North Point Light

Claiborne, when you get there, is found to be only a tranquil village on the shores of the bay, set in a sylvan perspective. It is a historical spot, however, and takes its name from that troublesome gentleman, William Clayborne, whose exploits in and about Kent Island are a well-authenticated matter of history. We call Clayborne a gentleman, but we do this only because he himself put "Gent." after his signature when signing it. We are not so sure he was a gentleman in the proper sense of the word. The village that bears his name, however, is attractive to those who have an eye for natural beauty. A number of summer-boarding houses have their being in and around the place, and in summer many aliens swell the

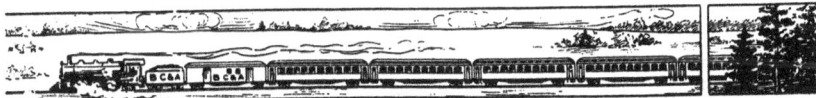

Claiborne populace considerably above its normal size and lend their gaiety to the community, which is, indeed, quite acceptable to it. And the Claiborne community is also quite as acceptable to the vacationists who frequent it. The writer enjoys the acquaintance of many persons who have grown fond of Claiborne as a vacation resort, and we take pleasure in recommending it. In any event, don't miss the Claiborne Cruise in 1913.

ᛈ   ᛈ   ᛈ

A Popular Vacation Pastime

The Eastern Shore

A Garden of Abundance---Famous for the Hospitality of
Its People---A Region Teeming With Delights
for the Vacationist--Where Summer
Breathes a Promise.

That wonderful peninsula between the Chesapeake Bay
and the Atlantic Ocean, commonly called the "Eastern
Shore," has long been famous for many things. Of agricultural and horticultural products it yields an abundance, an
ever-increasing abundance; of oysters, fish, and crabs its
yield probably leads any other similar locality in the world;
of people good and great it has produced many. It is a
region rich in history and traditional lore, to be expected in

a community whose settle-
ment was among the earliest
in America. Its climate is
tempered by the Gulf
Stream to such an extent
that the Southern extremity
is almost semi-tropical.
Here summer breathes a
promise to the vacationist.
Eastern Shore homes, fields,
woods, and waters teem with
delights for the toilers from
town. In dozens of homes
and hotels the natives open
their arms to the vacationist in a way which at once
brings him into harmony
with his strange environ-
ment.

The writer once overheard a Baltimore woman say that
the reason she so enjoyed spending her vacation on the
Eastern Shore was because she got such tempting things to
eat while there. To the average summer boarder, this
feature makes a strong appeal. It is of course true that
country folks "live better" from a gastronomic standpoint
than do their city cousins of average means, the reason
therefor being too obvious to call for discussion here; but
on the Eastern Shore this feature of their living is rather
more pronounced, we believe, than in many another locality.
Though famous as the habitat of the diamond-back terrapin,
Eastern Shore folks have long served this famous delicacy
only on rare occasions. There is, we believe, an old law
among the Maryland statutes which prohibits a man from
feeding terrapin to a slave more than twice a week.
Needless to say, this law has long since lost its job, because

terrapin are now far too scarce and valuable to feed to servants.

Among the products of this favored section, strawberries make a leading crop. Tomatoes, peas, and sweet corn are grown in large quantities for canning. On the lower shore potatoes, white and sweet, are the principal crop, and millions of bushels are grown in a single season. Fruit-growing is on the increase. Not many years ago this region yielded immense quantities of peaches, but the production of this luscious fruit has greatly decreased and the apple has, in a great measure, supplanted it in the growers' affections.

From Claiborne to Ocean City the country traversed by the B. C. & A. Railroad is well supplied with hotels and summer boarding-houses. About many of them we have been able to obtain data, which have been embodied in the list to be found on page 39. This list is compiled with a desire to assist prospective vacationists, and in connection with which we think a word of advice is appropriate. As everybody

will admit, it is always desirable to have all arrangements for accommodations made in advance of one's going. It is well, therefore, to select those houses which seem to appeal to you most, and to communicate with them about such details as may be of particular interest to you and yours. Then you can choose the one best suited to your requirements and make your final arrangements prior to leaving home. The foregoing is given, of course, for the benefit of the inexperienced; older heads will need none of our advice along this line.

In that section of Eastern Shore served by the B. C. & A. Railroad are many progressive towns and budding cities. Among the larger are St. Michaels, Easton, Salisbury, and Berlin—all of which are important business centres in their respective communities. Each has its quota of hotels and private places of entertainment, and the inducements offered the vacationist are varied and worth while.

These Eastern Shore towns, all of them, are attractive places to live or to spend awhile. They are hustling and ambitious. In fact, their ambition has been unjustly criticised. Of Salisbury it has been said: "A little burg with her face all scarred up from encounters with ill-advised aspirations." At the time this was said of Salisbury, her streets were all torn up and her natural beauty for a time marred by her heroic attempt toward having smooth, paved streets. But let the facetious gentleman above quoted visit the town now, and he will find conditions very much as they should be, with the scars beautifully healed. Salisbury, among other things, is noted for its fine homes. Here the residents seem to vie with one another in the pretentiousness of their residences, many of which delight the eye with their symmetry of proportion and mellow beauty and bespeak a well-developed artistic sense for their owners.

꘎   ꘎   ꘎

Little Voyages

Famous Inland Water Trips That Appeal to Everybody— Clean, Comfortable, Well Ventilated State Rooms— Excellent Cuisine—Courteous Officers and Attendants—Small Cost.

There are ever so many people who, for one reason or another, cannot see their way to take an ocean voyage. Europe may beckon in summer; in winter, Cuba and the Canal. Or, it may be that their longing tends toward nothing more oceanic than a coastwise trip with only two or three days at sea. It matters not the specific variety of ocean voyage that may be the beacon of your dreams, if you find its indulgence impossible what are you going to do about it?

Did it ever occur to you that if you were to look about you, you might find a very desirable substitute for that ocean voyage you have long sought to take? It has to precious few. So, apropos of the foregoing, we shall tell you briefly of a few delightful summer cruises—Little Voy-

ages—on salt water, which are near at hand, and very economical in both time and money.

While speaking of these trips in a general way, we want to tell you how popular they have become in past few years. Many persons take these trips year after year, sometimes making more than one in a single season. Indeed, they are becoming an annual event in the itinerary of an ever increasing number of pleasure-seekers. Some folks who have only a few days vacation, spend the entire time in this manner. It is travel, rest, and pleasure—all at the same time and for the same price. It is education, too. It gives one an opportunity to visit some near-home historic places, making the trip profitable and instructive. For teacher and student, business man and cultured scholar, these trips are designed to please—do please. Probably none is more pleased than the school boy or girl. They see something new and interesting almost every minute. It is a moving-picture of the most varied type.

The time required to make these trips, ranges from 36 hours to 4 days, depending entirely upon the trip you select. The prices vary accordingly, depending somewhat upon the type of accommodations desired. In arranging the details of a little voyage, call on or phone the Passenger Department, Pier 1, Pratt St., and they will take pleasure in working out the details of the particular trip you have determined to take, reserving suitable accommodations for your use, advising date of sailings, etc. We are not giving this sort of information here, because, as this matter is prepared several months in advance of the season, we cannot safely anticipate schedules, or even rates. This information will be gladly furnished, however, upon request.

TO THE WICOMICO, SALISBURY, AND OCEAN CITY.

A very desirable trip and a very popular one is the "Baltimore-to-Salisbury" route. Not only is it popular as a "little voyage" for tourists, but of late it also has become a popular thoroughfare to Ocean City. The advantages in reaching Ocean City via this route, instead of going via Claiborne, are obvious enough to those who are at all familiar with travel to Eastern Shore points; but to those who are not, we will say that this route to Ocean City eliminates nearly sixty miles of the trip across the Eastern Shore peninsula. The time required, of course, is much greater, but then as it is so filled with delight and so comfortable withal, this feature is counted in its favor rather than otherwise. The writer personally knows a number of persons who prefer to go to Ocean City by way of the Wicomico line and Salisbury, thereby reducing the railroad end of their journey to thirty miles. Not only do they prefer it, but they actually follow the bent of their preferment whenever possible.

Besides the elimination of nearly sixty miles of the rail journey, the principal drawing-card is the night on the water. With a good, cozy, comfortable stateroom, delicious meals, and a very courteous and attentive crew, one finds the briny odors and cooling breezes of the Chesapeake Bay particularly inviting. Having enjoyed somewhat the hospitality so freely dispensed on the Steamer "Virginia," the author takes especial pleasure in recommending this trip. Whether it be as a means of reaching Ocean City, or as a means of treating oneself to a restful and refreshing outing, enters not into the premises at all. In either case this trip is a treat, and has long been considered so by many travelers,—proof positive of which is the fact that they say so themselves.

Steamer "Virginia," of this line, will in all probability leave Baltimore on Tuesdays, Thursdays, and Saturdays of each week at 5.00 P. M., arriving at Salisbury by nine o'clock the following morning. Passengers desiring to continue the trip to Ocean City, will have ample time to make the first east-bound train leaving Salisbury. For such passengers the B. C. & A. Railway Company provides a bus, fare free, for transfer across the town of Salisbury, and also for the transfer of baggage. Thus passengers may check their baggage through at Baltimore and have no further trouble with it till they arrive at Ocean City. As this is one of our heavy passenger routes, passengers desiring to travel this way

A Little Voyager

during the summer months will do themselves a great kindness if they will reserve their accommodations not less than one week in advance of sailing. This is a feature of your plans that should not be overlooked.

M   M   M

TO THE CHOPTANK RIVER,
TILGHMAN'S ISLAND, OXFORD, EASTON,
CAMBRIDGE.

With the new steamers "Dorchester" and "Talbot," built in 1912, on this line, truly you have an added incentive to make this trip in the summer of 1913. We have already said so much about the palatial appointments of these comfort purveyors, that we are beginning to wonder if folks think we are over-much proud of them. In any event, as we have covered this matter of steamers so thoroughly in a separate booklet, which may be had for the asking, it is our purpose here to forego dwelling at length on their attractions and, instead, to speak at some length on the historical and other interesting features of the Choptank River country. More especially do we want to tell you of Cambridge, sometimes called the "Queen City of the Peninsula." In truth, to tell you ever so little about the

early history of the Choptank country, we would have to speak of Cambridge; because here one of the earliest settlements was made, though not the first in the valley. It is said that the first settler in these parts was Anthony Le-Compte, a distinguished French Protestant, who, with a few friends, in 1659, entered the Choptank River and settled on the south bank at a place called Horn Point. It was not until 1684, however, that the Colonial Government passed an act granting the building of a town on the site of Cambridge. Work on laying out the new town was immediately undertaken by John Kirk, History tells us, and in 1687 the town became the county-seat.

So, from the foregoing, it appears that Cambridge is one of the very old towns of Maryland. Yes, and some relics of the olden times still linger here and there, impressive reminders of the glory of other days. Straughn Mansion, erected in 1728, we are told, is one of the old

A Cozy Stateroom

colonial structures of note. Wallace Mansion is another. Here lived Sir RogerWoolford, Lord Baltimore's Commissioner for this section of Maryland; and later the Goldsborough family,the father of the present Governor of Maryland having been born here. Still another of the old relics of the colonial period is "The Point," the oldest house now standing in Cambridge. It is said to have been built in 1719. The court records show that when this property was first purchased the consideration was "1000 pounds of good merchantable tobacco." Interesting enough this transaction sounds to us now. Another interesting point is the old jail where Rev. Freeborn Garretson, the first Methodist minister in Dorchester, was incarcerated in 1780, after suffering many indignities at the hands of the populace on account of preaching what was then a new doctrine—and in the olden days all new doctrines were considered objectionable without folks troubling themselves to investigate their teachings, which condition exists, to some extent, even now.

Cambridge is popular with many folks as a summer

resort. Oakley Beach Hotel is probably responsible for much of this popularity. It stands directly on the water front, and has a pier projecting 750 feet into the Choptank River, with a dancing-pavilion built over the water on one side. From the pier is afforded good bathing, boating, fishing, crabbing, and a glorious view across the Choptank, 2½ miles wide at this point.

The first steamboat cautiously picked its way into the Choptank River in 1830. It was the old steamer "Maryland." On account of the sand-bar that made out in front of Cambridge, landings were not made here in those days. Then the nearest stop to Cambridge was Castle Haven.

The latter place is no longer a landing for steamers, but it is a point of interest on the south bank of the river and attracts the attention of every tourist. The old mansion stands out in striking contrast against the background of green, and the setting is ever so picturesque. This beautiful country-place, which was long the home of Col. Wilbur F.

Jackson, is now owned by a wealthy New Yorker. Col. Jackson, we will add, was the father-in-law of Baltimore's present Mayor.

The Choptank Cruise will be found interesting and enjoyable. It is one of the favorites. Aside from the trip on the bay, the lower Choptank is broad and picturesque and alluring. Indeed, in the vicinity of Cambridge it has been likened, at sunset, to the Bay of Naples. On a calm summer afternoon and evening nothing is more delightful, truly, than a sail over the broad reaches of the lower Choptank and of its tributary, the Tred Avon.

A word about Tilghman's Island must not be omitted. Tilghman's is the first and last port of call on this line, and is quite popular as a summering place. A number of summer boarding-houses are located here and extend their generous hospitality to all who find Tilghman's agreeable. The salient features are principally of the water variety, such as salt-water bathing, sailing, rowing, motor-boating, oystering, crabbing, and fishing. Because the village is directly on the bay, it is admirably situated to afford the summer vacationist every pleasure of the "great outdoors." A list of Tilghman's boarding-houses will be found on page 40.

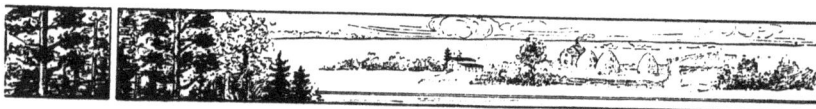

TO THE POCOMOKE RIVER
AND SNOW HILL.

Of the many summer cruises offered by the steamers of this company, the Pocomoke is not the least popular. Like every other line, it has its steadfast adherents, who remain loyal to their first choice year after year. Maybe it is their friendship for the big-hearted Captain of the "Maryland" that takes them on an annual pilgrimage to the river of black water. Be this as it may, the tourist who selects the Pocomoke trip for the summer of 1913 will, in all probability, return feeling that he has chosen wisely and well.

The name "Pocomoke" is taken from the Indian vernacular and means *black water*. The Pocomoke is a narrow, swift river, flowing through cypress swamps and marshlands, and its waters hold much alluvium in solution which is deposited at the mouth of the river. These deposits have formed a delta of soft mud at the river's mouth covering a large area, on top of which the water is shoal. Sometimes,

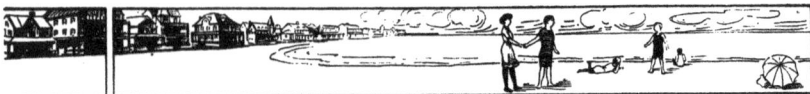

when the tide is low, it is a serious obstruction to navigation, but it in no way jeopardizes the safety of the steamers passing over it.

The climate of the country along and adjacent to the Pocomoke River is almost semi-tropical. In the springtime the flowers indigenous to this section bloom earlier here than anywhere else in Maryland. The most noticeable of these are the wild honeysuckle, wild rose, and the sweet-scented magnolia, which combine in lending a delicious fragrance to springtime's dreamy atmosphere. Their perfume is the delight of all tourists who travel on the river at this time of the year.

From the beginning the trip on the Pocomoke is a continuous unfolding of interesting details and genuine pleasure. A number of towns of considerable size and importance are touched,—Crisfield, Onancock, Pocomoke City, and Snow Hill, the terminus of the route. Crisfield is the greatest crab and oyster market in the world. Hundreds of crabbing boats have their rendezvous here, sailing out into Tangier Sound at sunrise and returning at sunset laden to the gunwales with the delicious crustacean. Onancock is on the Eastern Shore of Virginia, that country famous for its potatoes, excellent farming methods, and the wealth of its inhabitants. Pocomoke City, one of the leading towns of the Eastern Shore of Maryland, is the centre of a rich farming region, and is said to have an unusual number of hotels for a town of its size. Snow Hill is the county-seat of Worcester County, Maryland, and is the home of Maryland's senior U. S. Senator. It is at the head of navigation on the Pocomoke River, has twice-a-week steamer service with Baltimore, and also railroad service up the peninsula with Wilmington, Philadelphia, and New York.

The steamer "Maryland," which makes the trip to Pocomoke River and Snow Hill, is a comfortable, modern steamer equipped to take care of passengers in a most satis-

factory way. The state-rooms are well-ventilated, clean and wholesome; the saloon is attractively furnished; the dining-room satisfies the appetite of thousands of people in the course of a year and, we believe, is capable of gratifying the whims of the most fastidious who travel this way. As we have already pointed out, this trip has its admirers who come from a distance year after year to take the Pocomoke trip for an outing of three or four days. They thoroughly enjoy it, and bring their friends along to enjoy it with them.

Our Passenger Department, Pier 1, Pratt St., Baltimore, will be glad to give you any additional information desired, and to reserve accommodations for the trip.

TO THE OCCOHANNOCK RIVER
(EASTERN SHORE OF VIRGINIA)

Leaving Baltimore, Pier 1 Pratt St., twice weekly (Wednesdays and Sundays), the steamer for the Occohannock, usually the "Eastern Shore," provides a pleasure trip that is at once restful and interesting. Only a couple of years ago a gentleman from New England made the round trip on this line and pronounced it delightful—how delightful one can better tell by referring to the number of "Vogue" in which he told, in detail and at length, of the Chesapeake's charms and the interest attaching to the Eastern Shore of Virginia where touched by the Occohannock Line. The story referred to is profusely illustrated and makes good reading.

This trip takes one into the great potato country of the Eastern Shore peninsula. Here millions of bushels of both varieties are produced in a single season, and if the harvest be on when you make your trip, at every wharf on the line you will witness one great bulk of barreled potatoes—in some

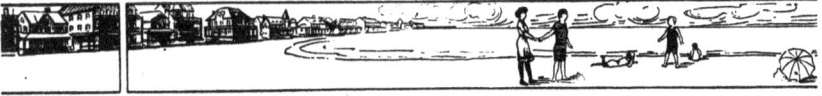

cases thousands of them—waiting for the steamer to relieve them of their burden. This section seems to be particularly well adapted to potato growing, and many farmers have grown rich from this crop. The harvest is earlier here than in many localities where potatoes are grown on a large scale, because of which the growers realize prices that make the crop extremely profitable.

On this line you'll find virtually all the delights of the typical Chesapeake Cruise. Aside from the summer-time attractions of the Chesapeake Bay and tributaries, you will find, within the ship's own precincts, every needful comfort to make your trip a pleasant one; and in the ship's dining-room your salt-air appetite is provided for in a tempting and substantial manner. The officers will be found hospitable, communicative, and well-informed.

This trip, both ways, requires two days and three nights.

Wachapreague, Va.

A resort said by those who have been there to be extremely attractive; situated on the brink where the famous Eastern Shore of Virginia is kissed by the Atlantic Ocean; with background of highly improved farm lands, luring forests and groves well flecked with the evergreens, pine, cedar, and holly; the great ocean unfolding before, and, only a little away in the rear, across a narrow peninsula, the Chesapeake, the world-famous Chesapeake; much gaiety out-of-doors, such as sailing, motor-boating, rowing, fishing, crabbing, automobiling, bathing; a large, comfortable hotel with a satisfying dining-room—this is Wachapreague in a nutshell, so far as the resort goes. The village roundabout we cannot speak of here.

The Piankatank Line

For a "way-down-the-bay" trip, probably none is more diversified in its attractions than this, and the traveler who

has a taste for the saltiest of salt air will doubtless find the Piankatank cruise quite satisfying. Instead of traversing the sinuous water courses of the Eastern Shore, this cruise is restricted entirely to the Chesapeake tributaries indenting the Western Shore of Virginia between the Potomac and Rappahannock and between the Rappahannock and York Rivers.

While lack of space prohibits our giving a detailed account of the ports of call, picturesqueness and attractive features generally, we can, however, recommend this cruise to be interesting, instructive, and enjoyable. The atmosphere down on the Piankatank is crisp with all the romance of the Chesapeake. Here summer's soothing solitude sends its call from a score of luring creeks and coves, and you want to linger awhile, you of the city's strife, and enjoy the charm of it.

The Nanticoke River Line

Between Baltimore, Md., and Seaford, Del., a steamer runs three times a week during the summer months, traversing the Chesapeake Bay and the Nanticoke River. For a pleasant little voyage that's just a little different, this is recommended. The sailings in former years have been on Mondays, Wednesdays, and Fridays of each week, but to verify the day of sailing, reserve staterooms, etc., communicate with the office of the General Passenger Agent, Pier 1, Pratt St., Baltimore.

ഄ   ഄ   ഄ

PRINCIPAL HOTELS AND COTTAGES AT Ocean City, Maryland

Name of Hotel or Cottage	Number of Guests	Name of Proprietor
Atlantic	500	
Avondale	25	G. B. Givans
The Breakers	50	Miss M. E. Newton
Brighton	75	Mrs. R. C. Quilin
Belmont	35	Mrs. W. T. Hearn
Congress Hall	100	Mrs. M. P. Kelley
Colonial	75	J. D. Wallop
Dennis House	50	Mrs. R. J. Dennis
Eastern Shore	50	Mrs. M. Taylor
Idlewild	25	Powell & Lankford
Gables	20	Mrs. L. W. Wyatt
Glendale	30	Mr. John J. Rayne
Hamilton	100	Mrs. J. L. Massey
Mt. Pleasant	100	Mrs. W. E. Buell
Mervue	40	
Mt. Vernon	50	Mr. J. D. Showell
New Avalon	50	Mrs. K. C. Hastings
New Windsor	75	Mr. Daniel Trimper
Nordica	50	Mrs. G. R. Bassett
Oceanic	75	J. D. Showell
Plimhimmon	200	Mrs. R. T. Shreve
Adams Hotel	50	R. B. Adams
The Rideau	50	J. H. Ellis
Sea Crest	15	
Seaside	150	
Tarry-A-While	25	
The Wetipquin	50	Mrs. F. J. Dashields
The Virginia	60	Miss M. P. Moore
Seabright	25	Mrs. Samuel Johnson
Fenwick		Taylor & Lankford

200 OTHERS ACCOMMODATING 15,000 GUESTS.

Inquiries for rates, etc., from Hotels whose proprietors are not named, should be addressed simply "Proprietor."

Baltimore, Chesapeake and Atlantic Railway Company

RAILWAY DIVISION

Name of Station	Name of Hotel or Boarding House	Rate per Week	Number of Guests	Distance from Station	Name of Proprietor	P. O. Address
Claiborne	Maple Hall	$ 7.00*	50	½ mile	Mrs. John Cockey	Claiborne, Md.
Claiborne	Little Haven	7.00*	50	¾ mile	P. Carroll Price	McDaniel, Md.
Claiborne	Bungalow	7.00	25	½ mile	Mrs. W. E. Cockey	Claiborne, Md.
Claiborne	Wades Point	7.00	80	¾ mile	Mrs. J. O. Kemp	McDaniel, Md.
McDaniel	Emerson Point	8.00*	50	½ mile	Mrs. J. T. Seth	McDaniel, Md.
McDaniel	Lewes Point	8.00	40	½ mile	Mrs. James H. Caulk	McDaniel, Md.
St. Michaels	Pleasure Point	6.00	50	8 miles	Mrs. J. C. Parlette	Neavitt, Md.
McDaniel	White Hall	6.00	25	4 miles	I. E. Kirkman	Wittman, Md.
McDaniel	Corrallton House	6.00	25	9 miles	Mrs. I. L. Bridges	Neavitt, Md.
McDaniel	Breezy Point	6.00	60	4 miles	Mrs. John B. Bridges	Bozman, Md.
McDaniel	Resurvy House	6.00	35	8 miles	Mrs. Mary C. Ball	Neavitt, Md.
McDaniel	Sandy Beach	5.00	40	3 miles	Mrs. Wm. T. Bridges	Bozman, Md.
McDaniel	Mansfield	6.00	75	3 miles	Mrs. Ida B. Neavitt	Bozman, Md.
St. Michaels	Wyatt House	7.00	35	¼ mile	Mrs. E. N. Ely	St. Michaels, Md.
St. Michaels		6.00	22	1 mile	Mrs. Paul F. Wallach	St. Michaels, Md.
St. Michaels		7.00	20	¼ mile	Mrs. M. Larrimore	St. Michaels, Md.
Royal Oak	Pasadena	8.00	100	½ mile	Frederick Harper	Royal Oak, Md.
Royal Oak	Oak View	7.00*	15	1½ mile	Mrs. Samuel C. Trippe	Royal Oak, Md.
Royal Oak	Chance Villa	8.00	60	1¼ mile	Mrs. Ormand Hammond	Royal Oak, Md.
Royal Oak	Solitude	8.00*	20	2 miles	Miss C. E. Hammond	Royal Oak, Md.
Royal Oak	White Hall	6.00*	30	2½ miles	Mrs. G. M. Brinsfield	Royal Oak, Md.
Royal Oak	Cedar Grove	7.00	100	¼ mile	Mrs. E P Hall	Royal Oak, Md.
Royal Oak	Sanfords Hermitage	6.00	15	4 miles	Miss Mary N. Denny	Royal Oak, Md.
Royal Oak	Pebble Beach	7.00	40	¼ mile	A. Boley	Royal Oak, Md.
Royal Oak	White Hall Farm	6.00	30	2½ miles	Mrs. C. M. Brinsfield	Royal Oak, Md.
Royal Oak	Retreat	7.00	30	1 mile	Miss Clara E. Benson	Royal Oak, Md.
Easton	Norris	12.00*	100	⅛ mile	W. K. Norris	Easton, Md.
Easton	Busby House	5.00	25	¼ mile	M. E. Joyner	Easton, Md.
Preston	Cox's Hotel	6.00	10	¼ mile	J. A. Cox	Preston, Md.
Mardella	Wilson House	5.00	5	⅛ mile	Mrs. J. W. Wilson	Mardella Spgs., Md.
Parsonsburg	Smiths	5.00	8	¼ mile	R. H. Smith	Parsonsburg, Md.
Berlin		5.00	10	1¼ mile	Mrs. E. B. Jacobs	Berlin, Md.
Berlin	Savage Hotel			200 yards	J. T. Savage	Berlin, Md.
Berlin	Atlantic Hotel			200 yards		Berlin, Md.

*Lowest rate. Higher rates for better accommodations

The Eastern Shore's natives are not satisfied with the mere preachment of hospitality; they have the courage of their convictions and actually practice what they preach.

SUMMER BOARDING-HOUSES

Baltimore, Chesapeake and Atlantic Railway Company

RIVER LINES

CHOPTANK RIVER LINE

Name of Wharf	Name of Hotel or Boarding House	Rate per Week	Number of Guests	Distance from Wharf	Name of Proprietor	P. O. Address
Tilghman	Faulkner House	$ 6.00	75	2 miles	Mrs. L. J. Faulkner	Fairbank, Md.
Tilghman	Fruit Farm	6.00*	50	2 miles	J. V. Harrington	Fairbank, Md.
Tilghman	The Rest	7.00	45	½ mile	Mrs. John T. May	Tilghman, Md.
Tilghman	River View	7.00*	30	¼ mile	Mrs. S. K. Wilson	Tilghman, Md.
Tilghman	Riverdale	6.00	100	¼ mile	Mrs. W. J. Jackson	Tilghman, Md.
Oxford	Tred Avon House	5.00	10	¼ mile	Mrs. James Paregoy	Oxford, Md.
Oxford	River View	8.00*	60	200 yards	James F. Fry	Oxford, Md.
Oxford	Fair View	6.00*	20	100 yards	Mrs. H. Bringman	Oxford, Md.
Bellevue	White Hall Farm	6.00*	30	1 mile	Mrs. G. M. Brinsfield	Royal Oak, Md.
Trappe	Carrollton	6.00	30	1 mile	E. F. Seymour	Trappe, Md.
Travers		5.00	12	6 miles	Mrs. C. M. Mitchell	Cambridge, Md.
Cambridge	Oakley Beach	8.00*	100	¼ mile	Capt. Jos. H. Neal	Cambridge, Md.
Cambridge	Patchetts	5.00*	30	¼ mile	Mrs. Fannie J. Patchett	Cambridge, Md.
Cambridge	New Dixon	10.00*	50	¼ mile	Mrs. J. B. Hopkins	Cambridge, Md.
Cambridge	Marvel House	5.00	40	¼ mile	Mrs. Daniel Marvel	Cambridge, Md.
Cambridge	Murphy's	5.00	26	¼ mile	Z. R. Murphy	Cambridge, Md.
Cambridge	Richardson's	5.00	20	¼ mile	Mrs. C. S. Richardson	Cambridge, Md.
Cambridge	Hotel Dorchester	8.00	75	¼ mile	Mrs. M. A. West	Cambridge, Md.
Denton		7.00	10	¼ mile	Mrs. H. E. Anderson	Denton, Md.
Denton	Fair View	5.00*	10	¼ mile	Mrs. S. M. Anderson	Denton, Md.
Denton	The Range	6.00*	10	3 miles	B. F. Somers	Denton, Md.
Secretary	The Chesdale	6.00*	40	2 miles	E. L. Hooper	E. New Mrkt., Md.

*Lowest rate. Higher rates for better accommodations

NANTICOKE RIVER LINE

Name of Wharf	Name of Hotel or Boarding House	Rate per Week	Number of Guests	Distance from Wharf	Name of Proprietor	P. O. Address
Bivalve	Hermon's		15	½ mile	Mrs. Jennie Hermon	Bivalve, Md.
Hurtts'	Brinsfield's	5.00	12	½ mile	Mrs. W. W. Brinsfield	Galestown, Md.
Sharptown	Ellis House	5.00	15	¼ mile	J. A. Ellis	Sharptown, Md.
Tyaskin	Tyaskin House	5.00	10	½ mile	A. S. Larmore	Tyaskin, Md.

OCCOHANNOCK RIVER LINE

Name of Wharf	Name of Hotel or Boarding House	Rate per Week	Number of Guests	Distance from Wharf	Name of Proprietor	P. O. Address
Harborton	Walker's	5.00	10	200 yards	Mrs. J. H. Walker	Harborton, Va.

Baltimore, Chesapeake and Atlantic Railway Company

RIVER LINES

POCOMOKE RIVER LINE

Name of Wharf	Name of Hotel or Boarding House	Rate per Week	Number of Guests	Distance from Wharf	Name of Proprietor	P. O. Address
Crisfield	Brick Hotel	$8.00	10	100 yards	Mrs. L. J. Tull	Crisfield, Md.
Crisfield	Palm Hotel	10.00	30	100 yards	Frank Gould	Crisfield, Md.
Crisfield	Crockett House	7.00	35	100 yards	W. W. Powell	Crisfield, Md.
Onancock	LeCatos	4.50	6	300 yards	Mrs. T. C. Bulle	Onancock, Va.
Onancock	Allen	5.00	6	300 yards	Mrs. M. S. Lecato	Onancock, Va.
Onancock	Island House	10.00	14	¾ mile	J. T. Hambrick	Onancock, Va.
		8.00	100	10 miles	A. H. G. Mears	Wachapreague, Va.
Pocomoke City	Townsends	5.00	20	300 yards	Mrs. J. B. Townsend	Pocomoke Cy., Md.
Pocomoke City	Ford Hotel	14.00	50	300 yards	S. J. Twilley	Pocomoke Cy., Md.
Snow Hill	Haywards	5.00	15	200 yards	Mrs. Thos. Hayward	Snow Hill, Md.

WICOMICO RIVER LINE

Name of Wharf	Name of Hotel or Boarding House	Rate per Week	Number of Guests	Distance from Wharf	Name of Proprietor	P. O. Address
Mt. Vernon	Bailey's	$4.00	12	1 mile	Mrs. F. E. Bailey	Princess Anne, Md.
Hooper's Island	Tyler's	7.00	10	6 miles	Geo. W. Tyler	Fishing Creek, Md.
Hooper's Island	The White	7.00	10	¼ mile	Mrs. Geo. H. White	Hoopersville, Md.
Hooper's Island	Lewis	7.00	10	5 miles	Wm. K. Lewis	Fishing Creek, Md.
Hooper's Island	Drummer's	7.00	10	5 miles	Mrs. Jas. A. Meade	Fishing Creek, Md.

PIANKATANK RIVER LINE

Name of Wharf	Name of Hotel or Boarding House	Rate per Week	Number of Guests	Distance from Wharf	Name of Proprietor	P. O. Address
Fleeton	Fleeton Hotel	$6.00*	20	¾ mile	R. C. Sanford	Fleeton, Va.
Harvey	Cobb Hall	6.00*	16	300 yards	Mrs. L. C. Harvey	Harvey's Whf., Va.
Cricket Hill	Hudgins	7.00*	50	⅞ mile	Clifford Hudgins	Cricket Hill, Va.
Warehouse	Casanova	7.00	10	¾ mile	John R. Landon	Cobbs Creek, Va.
Ocrans	Little Bay	7.00	40	3 miles	Jos. T. Yerby	Palmer, Va.

*Lowest rate.   Higher rates for better accommodations

Maryland, Delaware & Virginia Railway Co.

WILLARD THOMSON
Vice-President

T. MURDOCH
General Passenger Agent

General Offices:
PIER 1, PRATT STREET WHARF, BALTIMORE, MD.

—The invitation of the woods
The call of gleaming waters.

Rehoboth Beach Delaware

Where Pine and Brine are Ever Wooing--- Enjoys a Combination of Natural Advantages Unequaled --Well Supplied With Comfortable, Attractive Hotels and Cottages--- "Designed as a Place of Rest," one writer says.

The founding of that delightful resort known as Rehoboth Beach occurred about the year 1873. Its inception had to do with camp-meetings—the good old Methodist variety— and it is perhaps not unnatural that its founders should have recognized the obvious truism that a good camp-meeting site could hardly be a poor spot for a summer resort. Here on the Delaware coast this was especially true. Here a happy combination of conditions exists to enliven the days, yes, and nights of the summer seeker for sea-shore enjoyments. Much of this so called "happy combination" represents Nature's own handiwork; some of it, of course, has been fashioned by man.

Since a popular summer resort has grown up on this old camp-meeting ground beside the sea, a railroad has been built across the Eastern Shore peninsula of Maryland and Delaware, its seaboard terminus at Rehoboth, its western terminus at Love Point. From Love Point a ferry connects with Baltimore. Thus it is that a direct route has been established between Baltimore and Rehoboth Beach—a combined water and rail route with a combined length of 136

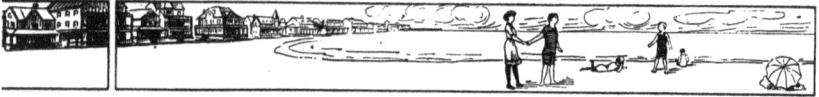

miles. It is such a pretty and delightful sail across the upper Chesapeake to Love Point! Only lasts two hours, to be sure, but then it is enough to add greatly to the spice of the journey. It is the same sail that is made by thousands in the afternoons during the summer merely for the pleasure of an outing where the air is pungent with salt and cool breezes blow. So much for the trip. We will now turn our attention to the modern Rehoboth and its attractions.

As one writer puts it: "One of the charms of Rehoboth lies in the fact that it is designed as a place of rest. The boardwalk has no noisy fakers or garish palaces where money can be exchanged for souvenirs. There is but one place where souvenirs can be bought and this establishment includes as well a candy store." The opinion of our esteemed contemporary is about right,—Rehoboth is designed as a place of rest. Still, there are many forms of innocent pleasure to call forth the energies of the vacationist. Chiefest of these, no doubt, is the Ocean Bathing.

Practically a universal fondness for ocean bathing is the foundation of all the enormous patronage and growth of American coast resorts. It is a diversion, a pastime, a form of exercise that is peculiarly fascinating, an appealing comfort on a hot day, and delightfully refreshing always. The charm of the bathing here at Rehoboth is due to no especial cause that we are aware of, but, broadly speaking, it is due to that same combination of conditions that delights one at virtually every resort on the middle Atlantic coast. It is a mingling with a formidable element of Nature that develops the pride of prowess; daily periods of luxuriating in the cool fragrant brine; the feast of feeding one's lungs on savory air, pure and pungent with salt. Of course, the ocean is

here and the beach is here, but then they are not unlike the ocean and beach elsewhere.

At Rehoboth the beach is not so broad as at Ocean City, but its quality is good and its slope gradual. Here the fast land makes out to within a few feet of the water's edge. This condition has its advantage. Rehoboth is not built on a sandy delta where green, growing things are aliens. Quite to the contrary, one finds here pretty streets lined with trees on either side; yards teeming with the beauty and fragrance of a wide variety of shrubbery and flowers; a miniature vegetable garden here, and a grass plat there. Such is the pleasing, restful, homelike appearance of the little Delaware resort.

As if to defend the town from the ravages of old ocean, a substantial boardwalk, 16 feet wide and a mile long (though we confess never to have measured it), trends the narrow strip of beach which here forms old ocean's brink. During the vacation season it resounds with the incessant pitter-patter of innumerable feet. Its functions are as varied as its functionaries are cosmopolitan. As a promenade, a thoroughfare for bicycles and rolling-chairs, or an impromptu drawing-room, it serves the summer colony equally well. Verily, a seaside resort is not a summer resort unless it possess a boardwalk, and we are glad to be able to announce that Rehoboth has a good one.

Aside from the superb bathing, there are many ways to amuse and enjoy oneself if "resting" grows monotonous. Here you will find skating rinks, dancing pavilions, moving-picture theatres, and bowling alleys; and fishing, crabbing, sailing, canoeing, etc., on Rehoboth Bay. With respect to the latter we think it fair to say that it is one of Rehoboth's

principal assets The bay is situated only about a mile from the Beach, entirely apart from the ocean save for a narrow inlet known as Indian Inlet. Its waters are shallow and calm at all times, and it is admirably adapted for sailing parties either by sunlight or by moonlight. The latter, of course, possesses a peculiar charm, especially for the young folks, but not more so, we suppose, than canoeing under the golden-orbed gentleman who so benignly blesses the earth with his borrowed radiance. The canoe, of course, has a delightful fascination for the heart of every romanticist— and most of us bear that stamp whether we know it or not. Those enterprising folks who like to reap some tangible reward from their activities, will find the bay an attractive fishing and crabbing ground. So, if you are imbued with piscatorial proclivities, if the tribes of fin and claw appeal to your gastronomical machinery, you will find here no signs to keep off the grass..

On the shores of Rehoboth Bay has grown up a little summer colony wholly apart from the main resort—a suburb, as it were, of Rehoboth the Great. Notable among the buildings in the little bay colony is the Y. M. C. A. club-house belonging to the Baltimore organization. Here many of the Baltimore Y. M. C. A. boys spend their vacation in a clean, jolly way. Every opportunity for the pursuit of out-door pleasure is afforded them here on the brink of this picturesque little bay, whose charm is accentuated, of course, by old ocean's magic presence so near to the eastward.

The great variety of hotels and cottages existent at Rehoboth for the care of the summer colony makes it impossible for us to go into details in mentioning this important item. We shall indulge rather freely in generalities in writing on this subject, and attempt nothing specific. The class of accommodations obtainable here will average up well with those which obtain at other coast resorts, barring, of course, the very pretentious and very costly. Rehoboth dosn't cater to the over-exacting. The appointments of her few hotels are not sumptuous enough to satisfy the ultra-fastidious taste. To be sure, everybody receives a cordial welcome in this nice old resort. Rehoboth needs the vacationist, and caste doesn't count much here where social distinctions are loosely drawn if at all. Fancy Rehoboth's natives differentiating among their summer guests. Their welcome is "for each and for all." They haven't yet acquired the gentle art of snobbery. But this is beside the mark a little. You will be more interested to learn that the town onjoys both electricity and gas for light and fuel; artesian water which analysis has shown to be exceptionally pure; an abundance of fresh fruit and vegetables from the nearby Delaware truck farms, whose wagons make daily visits to Rehoboth; and an atmosphere fragrant with salt and the balsamic savor of the encroaching pine forest. Numerically speaking, there are probably a dozen hotels and two score or more cottages open for the entertainment of summer visitors. The rates are reasonable here, owing to a combination of very acceptable conditions. Probably chiefest

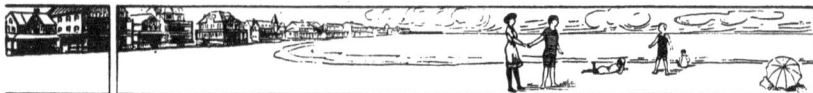

among them is one just mentioned,— the proximity of the nearby truck farms.

The number of churches at Rehoboth speaks well for its civilization. The array consists of Presbyterian, Episcopal, and two Methodist churches, and a Catholic parish.

We have already mentioned the nearby pine forest. It would probably be hard to reckon its value to the resort. A vast acreage of dense pines reaches to within a few hundred feet of the beach. Their rich fragrance pervades the air. Their cool vistas offer inviting paths for a stroll on a hot day. For a summer camp their shades are ideal. Indeed, a dozen bungalows have already obtruded themselves into these peaceful sylvan solitudes that reach out from the sea-brine toward the west. What a combination it is—this salt-air mingling with the breath of the pine forest!

In conclusion, it may be of interest to the prospective vacationist to know that many of the constituents of Rehoboth's summer colony own and maintain cottages here for their summer residence. Among these is the Nicaraguan Minister, besides other persons of note. These people reside here year after year during the summer months, which is in itself convincing evidence of the desirability of Rehoboth as a summer resort.

See list of hotels and cottages on page 72

Love Point

When Summer casts her magic spell of allurement over the country-side and Wanderlust builds her nest in your heart, the time has come to lay aside your busy-ness, fetch out your last summer's cap, and wend your way toward Light Street for a little cruise down the bay. Maybe the Love Point Trip will fill the bill. If so, then your trip will be across, rather than down, the bay.

For a short trip this has no superior in Chesapeake waters. The run down the river and across the bay takes just two hours, and another two hours to return. The stay at the Point is about three hours, giving ample time to eat supper at the Love Point Hotel, or for boating, bathing, fishing, or just resting on the shady lawn beside the lake. It is not necessary, of course, to eat supper at Love Point, as a good supper can be obtained in the dining-room of the good Steamer "Westmoreland."

As with all afternoon excursions, it is the trip on the bay, the salt-laden, breeze-blown billows of the Chesapeake,

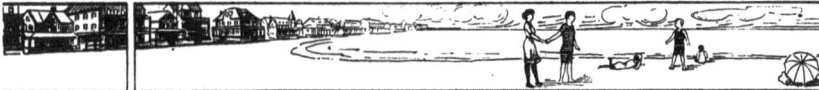

that is the really big feature of the Love Point Trip. So filled is the passage with new sights and new delights that one effortlessly forgets the cares that were left behind. The breeze is brisk and cool and refreshing. It gets next to your hide and makes you feel like a refrigerator. And, verily, such a feeling fills one with much joy on a hot day.

Coming home by moonlight is a joy that beggars description. Nor will we attempt to paint a picture so elusive. The pity is that the moon cannot be depended upon always to shine and kiss the waters with its mellow glow. However, laying all regrets aside, he is sure to shine on many a summer's night, and those young folks of a particularly romantic mien should wait on the Almanac and choose according to its dictates. Then the trip will surely be "adorable," as some of the girls say.

The northern extremity of Kent Island has been called Love Point nobody knows how long, and, indeed, it doesn't

Resting beside the Lake, Love Point

matter much. Tradition has it, some say, that an Indian love affair, ever so long ago, played a leading part in naming the "Sweetheart of the Chesapeake," as Love Point is often called. Whether this is true, we cannot tell; but we are convinced that Love Point is a lovely spot, a place that many of us love, and a beguiling place for lovers. Therefore, we are willing to believe it has the right name and deserves it.

The natural location, topography, and environment of Love Point are such that one wonders it was not chosen as a site for a down-the-bay resort long before it was. Lying close under the edge of the Eastern Shore and separated from it by a tiny sound called The Narrows, Kent Island extends from the Chester River on the north to Eastern Bay on the south. Love Point is the northern extremity of the island, and it is really a "point," with the waters of the Chester's broad mouth on one side and the Chesapeake's dream-waters on the other. This gives a splendid outlook either way. As to the Point itself, it looks pretty and cool and inviting on a warm day, though less sylvan than it once was. Time was when the outer portion of Love Point was largely covered with trees—a beautiful grove of them, with a trail leading into their labyrinthine depths. Then an enterprising real estate man hove to, attracted by the natural beauty of the place, no doubt, with the result that some of its rustic charm has given way to the more prosaic but useful haunts of the home-maker.

As a down-the-bay resort for the afternoon excursionist, Love Point has made its place in the hearts of many. Indeed, during the past summer many thousands made the trip to Love Point for an afternoon and evening's pleasure, grateful for an opportunity to flee from the dust and noise and care of city offices, banks, and stores. Indulgent husbands have found that for an outing for the wife and kiddies the Love Point Trip stands high, and the cost is trifling; and the young folks—well, it is hardly necessary to tell the young folks, because most of them know. And so the Love Point Trip we shall offer you during the summer of 1913 is backed up by the popularity of many summers. The attractiveness of the resort itself has received an uplift through the addition of more hotel room and a number of amusements. The fishing, crabbing, boating, and bathing were never better. And the trip across the breeze-swept waters of the grand old Chesapeake is a pleasure that calls for neither description nor praise.

As the exact sailing time has not been definitely settled, we ask our patrons kindly to consult the Baltimore papers for this information. Notice of the Love Point Trip will be published daily throughout the summer.

THE B. S. FORD   THE ANNE ARUNDEL   THE CALVERT   THE MIDDLESEX

LITTLE VOYAGES
On the Chesapeake Bay and Tributaries

Far and near one may look without finding a more magnificent system of inland waterways than the Chesapeake Bay and Tributaries. Besides being historically famous, these waters are wonderfully prolific of sea-food, offer endless luring trails for all sorts of water craft, and unfold a great panorama of scenery as interesting as it is diversified. If the Chesapeake Bay were in Europe—but it is not, so it is not much talked about.

When the first colonists came to Maryland and Virginia they thought the Chesapeake Bay a celestial place, and it is just as much so today. In fact, we are willing to stand sponsor for the statement that it has improved a trifle since then. Tourists through this country today do not have to fight their way as Captain John Smith did, nor subsist on his scanty rations. The watery paths he marked out are now followed in a different and better fashion.

These trips on the Chesapeake Bay and tributaries are becoming better known as time goes on. One that is somewhat more famous than any we have is the Baltimore-to-Washington trip, on what is known as the Potomac River Line. A sketch about it follows.

ᛒ   ᛒ   ᛒ

Oystering

Potomac River Line
(Baltimore to Washington)

Too much cannot be said in favor of the charms of the Chesapeake and of the great rivers that drain its basin. Of the many nice trips on these waters that are open to Baltimore and to Baltimore's visitors, one of the most attractive is from Baltimore to Washington, a delightful trip in summer on the Chesapeake Bay and the Potomac River. A popular trip it is, too, with stateroom accommodations sold out well in advance of sailing dates. The rush begins almost as soon as the weather warms up in the spring and lasts till the air takes on its autumn frost.

This trip just fits in with everybody's week-end, it seems. The tourist can leave either Baltimore or Washington on a Saturday afternoon, five o'clock, and arrive at the other of the two cities early Monday morning in time for business. The intervening two nights and a day are spent pleasantly on board the steamer.

Every necessary comfort is provided on the steamers of this line. They are modern and of a type that well suits the Chesapeake waters—a type that is typical of and belongs to the Chesapeake and its maze of tributaries. The moment

you open your stateroom door you are impressed with its cleanliness, neatness, and inviting appearance. No frills, to be sure, but you seem to feel at home, which is more important. You find beside your berth the electric button that brings the maid or bell-boy; another such button nearby gives life to the incandescent overhead; a basin, with running water, is in the corner. Such little things as tooth paste, talcum, and soap have been provided for your use in a little prize package marked "Colgate's," which sounds pretty good. And salt air, that great joy of water trips, is admitted through a window of pleasing proportions.

By the time you have wrestled with your over-packed grip and found the cheery checkered cap you brought along for deck wear, you discover that your steamer—your floating hotel, as it were—has been moving for sometime and that you're already well out in the lower Patapsco, nearing the Chesapeake. Then the jingle-jangle of a bell sounds somewhere amidship, echoing its plaintive music from stem to stern, and somehow instinctively you know that it means you are wanted in the dining-room.

Now, Chesapeake Bay colored cooks have long enjoyed some measure of fame. Every now and then some hefty scribe has taken a hand at lauding their achievements. So we'll suppress our eulogies for the moment till the lamp of enthusiasm burns low. Suffice it to say, however, that you aren't likely to be sad when you leave the dining-room.

These Baltimore-to-Washington steamers are noted for their ex-

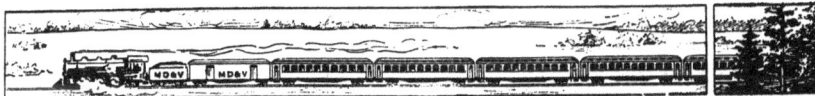

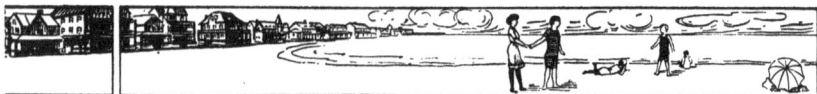

BUSHWOOD ST MARY'S CO MD

cellent meals. Lots of folks have had the agreeable experience of finding this to be a fact. A table d'hote meal,
including such relishable rations as oysters, soft crabs,
fried fresh fish, Maryland fried chicken, Maryland biscuits,
and all the et ceteras, all for a paltry sum—think of it! And
it is served up in good shape, too, in a way that tempts one's
appetite.

After supper you get out on deck pretty soon. The red
ball of the mid-summer sun sets, while you wait, beyond the
green hills of the Maryland shore-line in a blur of filmy
clouds. With its keen rays no longer dazzling your eyes,
you can make out the gray outline of the dome of Maryland's
Capitol, rising majestically above the sea of verdure that's
fast taking on the dark shadows of twilight. Annapolis lies
just to the westward, nestling among the low hills beside the
Severn. If your eyes are keen enough, you may be able to
peer through the deepening shadows and catch a glimpse of
the Nation's Naval Academy, where officers for the American
Navy are made to order.

In a minute the stars come out   A great moon, perhaps,
rises out of the breeze-blown water in the eastward distance.

So near its rising seems that it appears to come out of Pocomoke Sound, over to the eastward where the oysters come from. You recline amid the resiliency of your steamer chair, half dozing, half dreaming, drinking in the cool, salt-laden breeze that continually sweeps the ship's upper deck. Under such conditions one feels very much satisfied with one's little groove in human affairs. And the good ship plows on through the brine. She is not alone. Other steamers and all manner of sailing craft are encountered as the historic shores on either side slip hastily by.

At a late hour you crawl into your berth and the gentle roll of the waves soon rock you to sleep. You leave your stateroom window open and the pungent air of the bay pours in, its cool breath savoring of the sputtering spume outside. Such an atmosphere! And such sleep as one does have!

The dawn breaks, and your sleep breaks with it. The early morning finds you well in the mouth of the Potomac. All unconsciously, the good ship has veered from her sou'-

Mary Washington Monument
Fredericksburg, Va.

Monument to Leonard Calvert
St. Mary's City, Md.

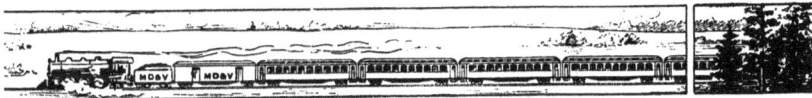

ward course and swung with effortless grace around Point Lookout and into the picturesque waters of the lower Potomac. You are surprised when you learn that you have really left the bay, so wide is the expanse of sparkling water that greets your eyes. "Four miles," the Captain says, is the width of the Potomac at this point, and, after looking it over, you are prepared to agree with him.

You recall that the "Ark" and the "Dove," carrying the first Maryland colony, sailed this same watery path nearly three hundred years before. You recall, too, that the first permanent settlement in Maryland was made nearby, at St. Mary's City. If you ask the Captain about it, he will tell you that the steamer made its regular landing at St. Mary's before day-break, but that if you make the return trip with him you will have ample time at the wharf to take a peep at the old church, the seminary, and the Cecil Calvert monument, all of which stand within a stone's throw of the landing.

The good steamer ploughs her way along, winding in and out of this creek and that, here a cove and there a baylet, "tying up" every little while at a wharf and sending ashore mail, express, and bales, boxes, and barrels of merchandise of indescribable variety. Sometimes only a few minutes are spent at a wharf, and sometimes an hour. This

One of the Joys of Vacation

gives the tourist an opportunity to go ashore and indulge in those antics that please him most. The writer has seen barrel races and similar "stunts" enacted, and often there is time enough to admit of a stroll along the luring trail of some shady country lane, the Captain agreeing to have the whistle "tooted" a few minutes before leaving-time. These stops at the numerous wharves also offer many opportunities to prove the "witchery of kodakery," as the Eastman people say, and find that it is good. To the younger generation of tourists the kodak has become an indispensable traveling accessory, almost as much so as that leathern Pandora box, the club bag. Indeed, it is our belief that no greater stimulus to travel exists today than the little black picture box with which everybody is familiar.

And so the day, in most cases a warm, sunshiny one, is spent in enjoying to the full the fresh air, the new sights, the loveliness of the nearby woods and wolds and waters when rejuvenated by summer's magic touch, the strangeness of the country wharf scenes, as, for instance, the use of oxen for drawing carts and wagons, which one would suppose had been abandoned long ago.

Washington is reached early, very early, the following morning, and if the tourist intends making the return trip by water, he has before him a whole day in which to take in the sights of the National Capital, and, as everybody knows, they are many.

Call or write our Passenger Department, Pier 1, Pratt St., Baltimore, for rates, reservation of state-rooms, etc., in connection with this very popular trip.

❧ ❧ ❧

The Ball Mansion, Rappahannock Valley

Rappahannock River Line
(Baltimore to Fredericksburg, Va.)

There is a certain amount of fascination in the thought of penetrating, by water, into the heart of "Old Virginia,"— a fascination born of traditions as old as American civilization. For some unapparent reason a feeling exists north and south, east and west, that Virginia is a place apart, a commonwealth within whose borders conditions are different, people are different, a difference akin to superiority. This popular impression, though marked, is only a vague mental halo that Time has woven about the Old Dominion, and is not to be taken too seriously. No doubt it is largely the outgrowth of the native pride, and the latter, of course, is well founded.

This cruise, or little voyage, on the Rappahanock River Line takes one into the very heart of Virginia, and, more-

over, into what probably ranks as its most famous valley,— the Valley of the Rappahannock. Here the superb scenery delights the eye and the eventful past delights the imagination. Luring creeks and coves make off inland through broad fissures in the river's banks, here low and marshy and there high and umbrageous. Into some of the largest of these creeks the steamer makes her way, and, rounding a bend, a little wharf is seen projecting from the fern-embowered shore. At many such the steamer ties up for a brief time, to land freight and passengers and perhaps receive others. And so the bustle of commerce goes on all day long, the steamer winding from one side of the river to the other, making landings in the most unexpected places.

From the standpoint of the pleasure-seeker, all these little incidents attending the commercial side of the trip are interesting enough; but the features which please him most, very likely, are the purity and pungency and coolness of the balmy summer atmosphere, the feeling of freedom that comes with this ideal life out-of-doors, the wholesome, appetizing meals that Chesapeake Bay colored cooks are famous for preparing. A trip of this sort affords a better means of living out-of-doors than camping out, because, while giving you the benefit of the out-door life, it still provides all the comforts of home,—a comfortable stateroom, spacious

saloons, and broad open decks, with an abundance of portable deck chairs to enable one to make himself quite comfortable in any portion of the ship, and canvas awnings to protect him from the sun. One can lounge on the decks in the open all day long, reading, day-dreaming, drowsing, and surveying the ever-changing scenery which unfolds, in a shifting panorama of loveliness.

The steamers "Middlesex" and "Lancaster" are expected to take care of the service between Baltimore and Fredericksburg during the summer of 1913. Both are quite comfortable and modern. While their appointments are not to be classed with those of the great Atlantic liner "Olympic" and similar ships, where the last word in sumptuousness has been attained, still we can truthfully say that the staterooms, saloons, and other passenger accommodations on these steamers are thoroughly comfortable and fully equal to those of the average hotel. Everything is clean, linen immaculate, saloons tastefully furnished, and "silver and fine linen" are much in evidence in the dining-rooms, but not, however, to the exclusion of tempting food.

The Rappahannock Valley is rich in historical associations, and many old landmarks, hoary with age, still remain

to cast shadows of the olden times on the sun-kissed paths of the present. Here and there they stand, now the ruins of an old church, now the stately lines of a well-preserved mansion of colonial design; and again sometimes it is just a monument, or an old barn shot through and through by a cannon-ball. The Captain or other officer of your steamer can point out numerous places of interest as you wend your way up the river, if you will but ask him. The story of "King" Carter, who was among the first to settle in the Northern Neck of Virginia, and of old Christ Church, which he built, and which can still be seen near Irvington, is especially interesting. Monaskon is also a point of considerable interest, in that it was the girlhood home of Mary Ball, who later became Mary Washington, mother of the illustrious George. There are a number of fine old colonial homesteads, too, to be seen on the river, each with its little story filled with heart-interest and sometimes a thrill.

Wharton Grove Camp Meeting, Rappahannock River

When Fredericksburg is reached the voyager will find himself in a little city teeming with interest, dignified, quiet, and quaint. He will find it inhabited by a people who are proud of their city and proud also of the part it has played in history. Here you will find old, dilapidated houses, apparently useless and a blot on the landscape, but withal the recipients of a wonderful amount of veneration. You wonder why, till you are told that some celebrity of the long ago once lived here, or perchance just stopped off for a few days and contributed the glory of his presence to the place to render it awesome to posterity. And so you proceed to be awed.

One such place is the old house near the railroad station known as the John Paul Jones House. The Admiral never really resided permanently in Fredericksburg, we are told, but it appears that in this house his brother, William Paul, lived and conducted a grocery, and the Admiral just happened to drop in once unexpected, as one's relatives often do, for a visit of indefinite length. Forthwith the fame of that house was established, and little love spots were etched in the hearts of the people. In St. George's Churchyard, Fredericksburg, will be found a much-scarred tombstone marked simply, Wm. Paul, 1774.

Compared with other American towns, this is an ancient burg. The actual founding of Fredericksburg occurred in 1679, though its legal establishment was not consummated till 1727. As early as 1608, History tells us, Capt. John Smith ventured as far as the falls of the Rappahannock, just above Fredericksburg, where he had a severe battle with the Indians. No attempt to establish a town was made, however, till many years later.

The fact that George Washington, when a mere child, attended school in Fredericksburg, and that his father, Augustine Washington, was appointed, in 1742, one of the town trustees, is information that should interest every true

American. President James Monroe, too, was a resident of Fredericksburg at one time, and his old home may still be seen on Princess Anne Street.

Marye's Heights Battlefield, the scene of such hard fighting and fearful carnage during the Civil War, is just outside of Fredericksburg and is one of the principal points of interest.

A day or two can be spent very pleasantly in Fredericksburg, though the tourist may not enjoy the acquaintance of any of its genial inhabitants. It is a quaint old town, and historical to a degree that renders it particularly attractive to the writer and scholar.

So attractive is the Valley of the Rappahannock that the inevitable has occurred. Western and Northern capitalists have provided themselves with large property holdings here and are developing them along progressive lines. One such is Mr. Alexander Berger, whose daughter is the daughter-in-law of that peerless Democrat, William Jennings Bryan. Mr. Berger has bought a large tract of land in what is known as Moss Neck, not many miles below Fredericksburg, and expects to establish an agricultural colony here. Another is Capt. J. F. Jack, of Los Angeles, Cal., who, a few years ago, bought a large tract of land at Port Conway, which he has converted into an alfalfa ranch. Mr. Jack himself is still a resident of California, and his manager takes care of his interests in Virginia. Still another who has capitulated to the charm of the Rappahannock Valley is Dr. Kilmer, founder of the Swamp Root medicine business at Binghampton, N. Y., who has surrounded himself with a very fine estate at Urbanna, Va. It is indeed gratifying to note that capitalists of the much-boosted West have begun to recognize the wonderful opportunities awaiting rightly directed capital and energy in this beautiful valley.

◻   ◻   ◻

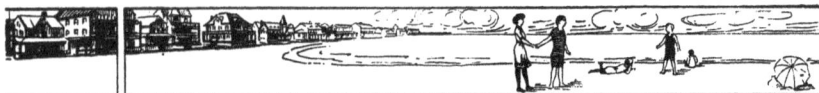

Patuxent River Line

In the past we have not said over-much about the Baltimore-Patuxent trip, although it would be hard to say why. Maybe it was because we operate so many lines on the Chesapeake Bay and tributaries that this one, not being of such proportions as some of the rest, got rooted away from the trough, as grandfather used to say. However that may be, so many expressions of praise have reached us in the last year or two that we have made a covenant with ourselves to treat the Patuxent route, in future, with generous doses of publicity.

Despite our rather shocking neglect, the quaintness and charm of the Patuxent River country has spread abroad rather more than many imagine. For example, somebody who knew prattled about it into Mr. Herbert L. Satterlee's ear, and Mr. Satterlee went forthwith and bought a wonderfully old and historic estate on the banks of the Patuxent. Of course the natives are overjoyed at having Mr. Satterlee

among them, because, as everybody knows, he is the son-in-law of that famous Wall Street money merchant, Mr. J. Pierpont Morgan, who is said by Mr. Pujo to have all the money bottled up. Mr. Satterlee's estate is at Sotterley Wharf and bears the same name. It was once the home of Governor Plater, second Governor of Maryland after the establishment of the state government, and consists of about six hundred acres of land and a magnificent old colonial mansion built in 1730. The latter Mr. Satterlee expects to restore, it is said, so that it will appear just as when Governor Plater occupied it.

And so the good news about the Patuxent country is spreading abroad. Slowly but surely it is stealing into men's hearts and compelling attention. A great country for the rich man is this, but it is even greater for the poor man, if he will work.

And for the vacationist—what? Attractive country homes with broad lawns and plenty of shade; hospitality that knows no equal; good, plain food in abundance; and no end of boating, crabbing, and fishing. The bay-shore may be more attractive to some than on the river. On the bay-shore are Fair Haven, Governor's Run, Dare's, and Plum Point wharves. Each has its summer colony—its colony of vacationists—and to a considerable number, no doubt, each proves "the beacon of their dreams."

The steamer to Patuxent River is one of our newest steamers, and is modern in every respect. She is thoroughly comfortable for passengers, well supplied with staterooms, and is manned by a capable, courteous crew. As a pleasure trip little voyages on this line are growing in popularity, and certainly there are many reasons why this should be so. From the standpoint of scenery, the Patuxent River route is not behind any of the Chesapeake steamer routes. Recently a party of prominent Philadelphia gentlemen were making the Patuxent trip, and while on St. Leonard's Creek, just off the Patuxent, one of their number, a widely traveled

man, remarked that the scenery here was the most sublime he had ever witnessed. His remark was not overheard by the writer, but one who was present and heard was good enough to break the news.

We can recommend this trip as a suitable one for your 1913 itinerary.

A BOATING PARTY ON THE CHESTER RIVER

Chester River Line

Though a short trip the Chester River route is just a little different from any of the others. From Baltimore to Chestertown is scarcely more than half a day's traveling, and inasmuch as the trip over is made one day and the return trip the next, it becomes little more than a short excursion.

The Chester River Line touches some of the principal towns on the Eastern Shore. Rock Hall, so handy to Baltimore and a noted place for summer boarders, is the first stop on the outbound trip. The town and outlying community are attractive for this sort of thing. The location is ideal in that it overlooks the Chesapeake, and presents every opportunity for those out-door sports that are sought for by

almost every summer vacationist. Here the fishing, crabbing, sailing, rowing, and bathing can be had for the taking, and one may spend his vacation in either an easy or a strenuous manner, as desired.

Queenstown, the colonial county-seat of Queen Anne County, is touched soon after the river is entered. It is one of the really old towns of the Shore, and is in the heart of a rich farming country.

Centreville, the present county-seat, ranks well among the larger towns on the Shore in point of attractiveness. Besides being a great local business centre for a large and productive farming area, it is essentially a town of beautiful homes.

Still further up the river is Chestertown, the county-seat of Kent. Chestertown has a reputation for hospitality, as, indeed, has all the rest of the Chester River country. It is also one of the oldest settlements on the Shore. The many fine buildings, churches, and homes which obtain here indicate a most prosperous community. Washington College is one of its principal assets.

A list of the boarding-houses along the Chester River will be found on page 74.

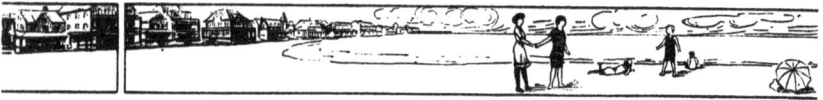

PRINCIPAL HOTELS AND COTTAGES AT Rehoboth, Delaware

MARYLAND, DELAWARE AND VIRGINIA RAILWAY COMPANY

Name of Hotel or Cottage	Number of Guests	Name of Proprietor
Henlopen Hotel.........	250	.........Walter Burton
Seaside Cottage..........	150	...........M. Rathhouse
Hotel Brayton	150	.......Sussex Trust Co.
Hotel Windson..........	150	............L. T. West
Windermere............	100	....Mrs. Virginia Taylor
Bell Haven by-the-Sea....	150	........Robert Hinckley
Menqua	75	.......Mrs. V. S. Collins
Shock Cottage..........		.......Mrs. W. Barnett
Garage Parlors.........		.....Mrs. L. T. Carmine
Sea View Cottage........		......Mrs. M. B. Day
Burton Cottage.........		.........Mrs. Burton
Rest Cottage...........		......Mrs. M. W. Smith

In addition to the hotels named above are a number of private cottages, where accommodations may be had at reasonable rates for two or three persons.

A FEW HOTELS AND BOARDING-HOUSES ON THE RAILWAY DIVISION OF THE

Maryland, Delaware and Virginia Railway Company

Name of Station	Name of Hotel or Boarding House	Rate per Week	Number of Guests	Distance from Station	Name of Proprietor	P. O. Address
Love Point	Love Point Hotel	$ 8.00*	100	50 yards	Capt. J. F. Legg	Love Point, Md.
Stevensville	Lowery's	7.00	14	¼ mile	Mrs. F. M. Jackson	Stevensville, Md.
Chester	Chester View	6.00*	13	½ mile	Mrs. Julia E. White	Chester, Md.
Chester	Shamrock Inn	6.00*	15	½ mile	Henry A. Walters	Chester, Md.
Chester	Fishermen's Inn	14.00	25		C. J. B. Mitchell	Chester, Md.
Winchester	Ireland House	4.50	10	¼ mile	Mrs. Edward Ireland	Ford's Store
Narrows	Wayside Inn	6.00	15	¼ mile	Mrs. Cora Gardner	Chester, Md.
Centreville	Winton	8.00	20	4 miles	Mrs. Katie Story	Centreville, Md.
Centreville	Arlington	7.00*	100	¼ mile	H. M. Gilbert	Centreville, Md.
Hillsboro	Hillsboro Hotel	7.00*	40	¼ mile	G. Smith	Hillsboro, Md.
Tuckahoe	Elms Farm	4.00	8	300 yards	J. C. Spicker	Tuckahoe, Md.
Hickman		3.50	4	4 miles	W. T. Hignut	Federalsburg, Md
Hickman		4.00	10	¼ mile	J. T. Breeding	Hickman, Del.
Lewes	Ocean House	7.00*	75	½ mile	Clarence Beebe	Lewes, Del.
Lewes	Hotel Rodney	8.00	20	½ mile	Geo. H. Buchannan	Lewes, Del.
Queenstown	The Linden	8.00	25	¼ mile	S. E. Kirby	Queenstown, Md.
Denton	Rosedale	5.00	18	¼ mile	Mrs. M. F. Johnson	Denton, Md.
Denton		5.00	10	¼ mile	Mrs. H. E. Anderson	Denton, Md.
Denton	Fair View	5.00	10	¼ mile	Mrs. S. M. Anderson	Denton, Md.
Denton	Walker	5.00	10	¼ mile	Mrs. N. J. Walker	Denton, Md.
Denton	Butler House	5.00	10	¼ mile	Miss Caroline Butler	Denton, Md.
Denton	The Range	6.00	16	2½ miles	B. F. Somers	Denton, Md.
Denton	Brick Hotel	7.00*	40	½ mile	J. T. Wright	Denton, Md.
Greenwood	The Eagle	10.00	20	¼ mile	Chas. C. Short	Greenwood, Del.
Ellendale	The Bright	7.00*	15	¼ mile	J. H. Jester	Ellendale, Del.

PATUXENT RIVER LINE

Solomons	Locust Inn	$ 6.00	20	¼ mile	Geo. W. Condiff	Solomons, Md.
Solomons	Pt. Patience	7.00*	35	1½ miles	Mrs. F. P. Marsburger	Solomons, Md.
Solomons	The Maples	7.00	20	¼ mile	Mrs. W. H. Marsh	Solomons, Md.
Plum Point	Dixon's	5.00*	10	100 yards	Mrs. J. A. Dixon	Plum Point, Md.
Benedict	New Era	5.00	8	100 yards	M. T. Johnson	Benedict, Md.
St. Leonards	Cedar Dale	6.00	6	2 miles	Mrs. James Broome	St. Leonards, Md.
Dukes	Sheridan Point	6.00	25	150 yards	Mrs. Wm. F. Dowell	Adelina, Md.

*Lowest rate. Higher rates for better accommodations

CHESTER RIVER LINE

Name of Wharf	Name of Hotel or Boarding House	Rate per Week	Number of Guests	Distance from Wharf	Name of Proprietor	P. O. Address
Rock Hall	Shirley Larm	$ 6.00	50	6 miles	Mrs. Rich'd B. Willson	Rock Hall, Md.
Queenstown	Queen Cottage	6.00	35	20 yards	Mrs. W. W. Story	Queenstown, Md.
Queenstown	Forest Lodge	8.00	12	¾ mile	Mrs. M. E. Davidson	Queenstown, Md.
Queenstown		5.00*	6	¼ mile	Mrs. S. C. Jones	Queenstown, Md.
Queenstown	Harbor View	8.00	10	¼ mile	Mrs. J. Fred Holden	Queenstown, Md.
Queenstown	Central		14	¼ mile	Mrs. Jos. Sparks	Queenstown, Md.
Bogles	Trumpington Manor	6.00	35	3 miles	Mrs. J. R. Ringgold	Rock Hall, Md.
Bogles	Mt. Windom	5.00	50	2½ miles	Mrs. P. A. Willson	Rock Hall, Md.
Chestertown	Imperial	7.00*	30	¼ mile	Jos. R. Lambert	Chestertown, Md.
Chestertown	The Abbey	7.00	20	¼ mile	Mrs. M. P. Finley	Chestertown, Md.
Crumpton	Maple View	7.00	10	¼ mile	Mrs. D. V. Cresswell	Crumpton, Md.
Crumpton	Maple Shade	5.00	10	¼ mile	Mrs. Thos. G. Jarman	Crumpton, Md.
Crumpton	River View	8.00	3	20 feet	Mrs. Wm. G. Foulks	Crumpton, Md.

POTOMAC RIVER LINE

Name of Wharf	Name of Hotel or Boarding House	Rate per Week	Number of Guests	Distance from Wharf	Name of Proprietor	P. O. Address
Millers	Curleys	$ 7.00	50	½ mile	Wm. E. Curley	Ridge, Md.
Millers	The Dunbar	8.00	40	½ mile	W. W. Dunbar	Ridge, Md.
Millers	Raleigh	7.00	50	¼ mile	Mrs. M. M. Curley	Ridge, Md.
Coan	Rice Hotel	6.00	25	3½ miles	J. G. Rice	Heathsville, Md.
Lewisetta	Chesapeake	6.00*	45	¼ mile	Geo. W. Thomas	Lewisetta, Md.
Piney Point	Piney Point	7.00*	175	¼ mile	Warren Tolson	Tolson, Md.
Piney Point	Swanns	7.00	70	1 mile	J. T. Swann	Piney Point, Md.
Piney Point	Traver's Retreat	6.00	15	½ mile	Mrs. P. M. Pettit	Piney Point, Md.
Leonardtown	St. Mary's	8.00*	200	¼ mile	J. R. Duke	Leonardtown, Md.
Bushwood	River Springs	8.00	100	3 miles	Robt. D. Blackistone	River Spgs., Md.
Lancaster	The Acton	9.00	10	⅛ mile	Mrs. S. Acton	Rock Point, Md.
Rock Point	Banks O' Th' Del	6.00	20	2½ miles	Mrs. Josephine Willett	Harris Lot, Md.

RAPPAHANNOCK RIVER LINE

Name of Wharf	Name of Hotel or Boarding House	Rate per Week	Number of Guests	Distance from Wharf	Name of Proprietor	P. O. Address
White Stone	White Stone Beach	$ 5.00*	20	200 yards	E. E. Hathaway	Taft, Va.
Millenbeck	Rogers	5.00	10	200 yards	Mrs. C. L. Rogers	Millenbeck, Va.
Urbanna	Nelson	8.00*	100	200 yards	D. M. Nelson	Remlik, Va.
Water View	Inglewood	7.00	10	¼ mile	Mrs. E. B. Davis	Waterview, Va.
Whealton	Whealton	6.00	14	¼ mile	John E. Goslee	Whealton, Va.
Sharps	Clarkson's	5.00*	14	100 yards	J. W. Clarkson	Sharps, Va.
Sharps	Simonson's	5.00	6	200 yards	Mrs. Lou Simonson	Sharps, Va.
Wellfords	Garland House	5.00	20	5 miles	W. H. Rice	Warsaw, Va.
Fredericksburg	Ray House	5.00	20	¼ mile	J. D. Ray	Fred'ksburg, Va.
Fredericksburg	The Enterprise	7.00*	30	¼ mile	Mrs. W. F. Coates	Fred'ksburg, Va.
Fredericksburg	Hotel Ferderick	12.50	75	¼ mile	W. R. Lucas	Fred'ksburg, Va.
Tappahannock	Monumental	6.00	20	¼ mile	Laura M. Gresham	Tappahannock, Va.
Tappahannock		10.00	25	¼ mile	J. F. Rahns	Tappahannock, Va.
Burtons	Burton House	6.00	50	¼ mile	Mrs. C. S. Burton	Urbanna, Va.
Burtons		7.00	8	1¼ miles	A. L. Jones	Urbanna, Va.
Burtons	Marie Springs	4.00	10	3 miles	Mrs. Weston Bristow	Stormount, Va.
Haymount	The Haymount	8.00	10	½ mile	Mrs. C. B. Conway	Moss Neck, Va.
Ottoman		6.00	25	¾ mile	Mrs. Geo. H. Steuart	Ottoman, Va.

*Lowest rate. Higher rates for better accommodations

ADVERTISING

SECTION

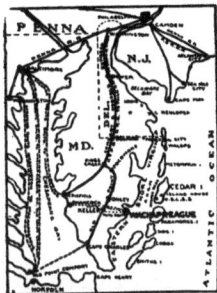

www.ingramcontent.com/pod-product-compliance
Lightning Source LLC
Chambersburg PA
CBHW052157090426
42741CB00010B/2311